D1460066

Best-Loved
JOYCE

JAMES JOYCE (1882–1941) is regarded as one of the most influential and important authors of the twentieth century. He was born into a middle-class Catholic family in 1882, in Rathgar, a fashionable suburb of Dublin. Joyce's early years were happy, and he was educated at Clongowes, Belvedere and University College Dublin, until his father's financial troubles led to the family's decline.

After graduating, Joyce went to Paris, though was recalled to Dublin in April 1903 due to the illness and subsequent death of his mother. Back in Ireland, he met Nora Barnacle, the Galway woman who was to become his wife and a major inspiration for his most famous work, *Ulysses* (1922).

In 1904 Joyce and Barnacle emigrated to continental Europe. During World War One, Joyce and Barnacle, and their two children, Giorgio and Lucia, moved to Zurich where Joyce began *Ulysses*. He returned to Paris for two decades, and his reputation as an avant-garde writer grew. He finished and published *Ulysses*, and later wrote *Finnegans Wake*.

In 1940, Joyce returned to Switzerland, where he and his family had been given asylum during World War Two. Due to complications after a stomach operation, he was to die there, at the age of fifty-nine, on 13 January 1941. He is buried in Fluntern cemetery, Zurich.

Joyce's works include the short story collection *Dubliners* (1914); novels *A Portrait of the Artist as a Young Man* (1916), *Ulysses* (1922) and *Finnegans Wake* (1939); two poetry collections *Chamber Music* (1907) and *Pomes Penyeach* (1927); and one play, *Exiles* (1918).

Dublin-based writer, JAMIE O'CONNELL teaches in University College Dublin and works for publishers Gill Books. His short fiction has been published in a number of journals, featured on RTÉ Radio, and he has read at many festivals and universities in Ireland, China, Spain and the USA. His work has been short-listed for the Maeve Binchy Award and the Sky Arts Future's Fund, and long-listed for BBC Radio 4 Opening Lines Short Story Competition. He is an editor of *The Dublin Illustrated Edition of Ulysses* (The O'Brien Press, 2014).

Best-Loved
JOYCE

selected by JAMIE O'CONNELL

Introduction by Bob Joyce

With illustrations by Emma Byrne

THE O'BRIEN PRESS
DUBLIN

First published 2017 by The O'Brien Press Ltd,
12 Terenure Road East, Rathgar, Dublin 6, D06 HD27, Ireland.
Tel: +353 1 4923333; Fax: +353 1 4922777
E-mail: books@obrien.ie; Website: www.obrien.ie
The O'Brien Press is a member of Publishing Ireland.

ISBN: 978-1-84717-839-8

Every effort has been made to trace copyright holders and to obtain their permission for the
use of copyright material. The publisher apologises for any errors or omissions and would
be grateful if notified of any corrections that should be incorporated in future reprints or
editions of this book.

The author and publisher gratefully acknowledge permission to include the following
copyright material:
Budgen, Frank, *James Joyce and the Making of Ulysses* © By permission of Joan Budgen.
Ellmann, Richard, *James Joyce* © By permission of Oxford University Press, USA.
Power, Arthur, *Conversations with James Joyce* © By permission of The Lilliput Press, Dublin.

Printed and bound in the Czech Republic by Finidr Ltd.
The paper in this book is produced using pulp from managed forests

Published in
DUBLIN
UNESCO
City of Literature

contents

INTRODUCTION

by Bob Joyce, grand-nephew of James Joyce

James Joyce departed Dublin for Trieste on the night of the 11 September 1912. He was never to return to the city he immortalised, the city of his birth. Before leaving, he asked his brother Charles (Charlie), my grandfather, to write to their other brother Stanislaus, telling him about his failed attempts to have *Dubliners* published. He appended the following note to Charlie's letter, explaining what was about to happen to the printed sheets of *Dubliners*:

The 1000 copies of Dubliners are to be destroyed by fire in the morning.

Jim

This was the last time that Joyce wrote on Irish soil. He was devastated and bitter due to his treatment by an Irish publisher and printer, so much so that he penned the poem *Gas from a Burner* on his way back to Trieste. Lines from this poem appear on page 60. It has to be remembered that he had spent three years writing his book of short stories *Dubliners* and seven years trying to have it published. This included a final failed attempt to have the book published

7

in Dublin by the Dublin publishing company Maunsel and Company. Maunsel's printer, John Falconer, stated that it was only when the book was set and printed that they had discovered what kind of book it was. He considered it objectionable and unworthy of publication. Joyce was in despair, thinking that his writings would never see the light of day. Little did he know at that time that he would succeed, not only in having *Dubliners* published, but that he would also have three further works published: *Portrait of the Artist as a Young Man*, *Ulysses* and *Finnegans Wake*. His writings would have a profound impact on English literature.

However, despite his celebrated status, readers find some of his work difficult. *Ulysses* is undoubtedly one of the most challenging yet rewarding novels ever published. As for *Finnegans Wake*, a reader once said, 'it's a pity that nobody has translated it into English!'

Best-Loved Joyce portrays the writer at his most accessible. Glimpses of the genius of Joyce abound with humour, love, pain and loss. The collection is filled with real gems that will inspire you to read his books. Here you have a wonderful opportunity to experience and enjoy a selection of quotations from Joyce's works, skilfully put together by Jamie O'Connell and published by The O'Brien Press. I particularly like the way the *Best-Loved Joyce* quotations are grouped under some of the emotions that Joyce displays in his writings.

You will find quotations from the short stories of *Dubliners*, the semi-biographical *Portrait of the Artist as a Young Man*, his masterpiece *Ulysses*, and his final novel *Finnegans Wake*.

In *Best-Loved Joyce* the artist and designer Emma Byrne draws the reader into James Joyce's words with her book design and beautifully constructed illustrations of Dublin in Joyce's time.

Joyce was a conjuror with words and captured the essence of all human life. *Best-Loved Joyce* will leave you with a sense of his humour and an insight into his Irish, and more specifically, his Dublin wit. He started writing as a poet, which is evident from many of the quotations chosen by Jamie O'Connell.

It is fitting that one of the quotations in the final section deals with life, joy, love and death – They lived and laughed and loved and left, or as Joyce put it in *Finnegans Wake*, 'They lived und laughed ant loved end left.' This is a remarkable sentence, condensing into a nutshell a galaxy of human civilizations.

Joyce asked the question: 'Is there one who understands me?' and stated: 'The demand that I make of my reader is that he should devote his whole life to reading my works.'

You are not expected to comply with his demand. Just let Joyce charm and disarm you!

truth

People could put up with being bitten by a wolf but what properly riled them was a bite from a sheep.

Ulysses

Rapid motion through space elates one; so does notoriety; so does the possession of money.

'After the Race', *Dubliners*

—You behold in me, Stephen said with grim displeasure, a horrible example of free thought.

Ulysses

Secrets, silent, stony sit in the dark palaces of both our hearts: secrets weary of their tyranny: tyrants willing to be dethroned.

Ulysses

The mocker is never taken seriously when he is most serious.

Ulysses

The sacred pint alone can unbind the tongue ...

Ulysses

Absence makes the heart grow younger.

Ulysses

Then as to money – he really had a great sum under his control … This knowledge had previously kept his bills within the limits of reasonable recklessness, and, if he had been so conscious of the labour latent in money when there had been question merely of some freak of the higher intelligence, how much more so now when he was about to stake the greater part of his substance! It was a serious thing for him.

'After the Race', *Dubliners*

A dream of favours, a favourable dream. They know how they believe that they believe that they know. Wherefore they wail.

Finnegans Wake

Thanks be to God we lived so long and did so much good.

A Portrait of the Artist as a Young Man

What was after the universe? Nothing. But was there anything round the universe to show where it stopped before the nothing place began? It could not be a wall; but there could be a thin thin line there all round everything. It was very big to think about everything and everywhere. Only God could do that.

A Portrait of the Artist as a Young Man

Thus the unfacts, did we possess them, are too imprecisely few to warrant our certitude

Finnegans Wake

Thought is the thought of thought.

Ulysses

... if it is thus, I ask emphatically whence comes this thusness.

A Portrait of the Artist as a Young Man

If you can put your five fingers through it, it is a gate, if not a door. Shut your eyes and see.

Ulysses

... too excited to be genuinely happy.

'After the Race', *Dubliners*

... the tall form of the young professor of mental science discussing on the landing a case of conscience with his class like a giraffe cropping high leafage among a herd of antelopes ...

A Portrait of the Artist as a Young Man

He laughed to free his mind from his mind's bondage.

Ulysses

—We were always loyal to lost causes, the professor said. Success for us is the death of the intellect and of the imagination.

Ulysses

Sleep, where in the waste is the wisdom?

Finnegans Wake

Be just before you are generous.

Ulysses

… Force, hatred, history, all that. That's not life for men and women, insult and hatred. And everybody knows that it's the very opposite of that that is really life.

—What? says Alf.

—Love, says Bloom. I mean the opposite of hatred.

Ulysses

The soul is born, he said vaguely, first in those moments I told you of. It has a slow and dark birth, more mysterious than the birth of the body. When the soul of a man is born in this country there are nets flung at it to hold it back from flight. You talk to me of nationality, language, religion. I shall try to fly by those nets.

A Portrait of the Artist as a Young Man

If we were all suddenly somebody else.

Ulysses

Kelly. Gerty Mac Dowell loves the ...

the elephant, loves Alice, the ...

except for ...

be sexual ...

is like ...

wonder ...

romance ...

I wish some man or woman ...

... heart in

... kiss ... and theres nothing like a kiss long and ...

roken already.

love **and** *romance*

Love loves to love love. Nurse loves the new chemist. Constable 14 A loves Mary Kelly. Gerty Mac Dowell loves the boy that has the bicycle. M. B. loves a fair gentleman. Li Chi Han lovey up kissy Cha Pu Chow. Jumbo, the elephant, loves Alice, the elephant. Old Mr Verschoyle with the ear trumpet loves old Mrs Verschoyle with the turnedin eye. The man in the brown macintosh loves a lady who is dead. His Majesty the King loves Her Majesty the Queen. Mrs Norman W. Tupper loves officer Taylor. You love a certain person. And this person loves that other person because everybody loves somebody but God loves everybody.

Ulysses

And you'll miss me more as the narrowing weeks wing by. Someday duly, oneday truly, twosday newly, till whensday.

Finnegans Wake

Your heart perhaps but what price the fellow in the six feet by two with his toes to the daisies? No touching that. Seat of the affections. Broken heart. A pump after all, pumping thousands of gallons of blood every day. One fine day it gets bunged up and there you are. Lots of them lying around here: lungs, hearts, livers. Old rusty pumps: damn the thing else. The resurrection and the life. Once you are dead you are dead. That last day idea. Knocking them all up out of their graves. Come forth, Lazarus! And he came fifth and lost the job.

Ulysses

What did that mean, to kiss? You put your face up like that to say good night and then his mother put her face down. That was to kiss. His mother put her lips on his cheek; her lips were soft and they wetted his cheek; and they made a tiny little noise: kiss. Why did people do that with their two faces?

A Portrait of the Artist as a Young Man

Her antiquity in preceding and surviving successive tellurian generations: her nocturnal predominance: her satellitic dependence: her luminary reflection: her constancy under all her phases, rising, and setting by her appointed times, waxing and waning: the forced invariability of her aspect: her indeterminate response to inaffirmative interrogation: her potency over effluent and refluent waters: her power to enamour, to mortify, to invest with beauty, to render insane, to incite to and aid delinquency: the tranquil inscrutability of her visage: the terribility of her isolated dominant implacable resplendent

propinquity: her omens of tempest and of calm: the
stimulation of her light, her motion and her presence: the
admonition of her craters, her arid seas, her silence: her
splendour, when visible: her attraction, when invisible.

Ulysses

A wave of yet more tender joy escaped from his heart
and went coursing in warm flood along his arteries. Like
the tender fire of stars moments of their life together,
that no one knew of or would ever know of, broke upon
and illumined his memory. He longed to recall to her
those moments, to make her forget the years of their dull
existence together and remember only their moments of
ecstasy. For the years, he felt, had not quenched his soul
or hers. Their children, his writing, her household cares
had not quenched all their souls' tender fire. In one letter
that he had written to her then he had said: "Why is it that
words like these seem to me so dull and cold? Is it because
there is no word tender enough to be your name?"

Like distant music these words that he had written years
before were borne towards him from the past. He longed
to be alone with her. When the others had gone away, when
he and she were in the room in the hotel, then they would
be alone together. He would call her softly:

"Gretta!"

Perhaps she would not hear at once: she would be undressing. Then something in his voice would strike her. She would turn and look at him …

'The Dead', *Dubliners*

White roses and red roses: those were beautiful colours to think of. And the cards for first place and second place and third place were beautiful colours too: pink and cream and lavender. Lavender and cream and pink roses were beautiful to think of. Perhaps a wild rose might be like those colours and he remembered the song about the wild rose blossoms on the little green place. But you could not have a green rose. But perhaps somewhere in the world you could.

A Portrait of the Artist as a Young Man

She leaned for a moment on his arm in getting out of the cab and while standing at the curbstone, bidding the others good-night. She leaned lightly on his arm, as lightly as when she had danced with him a few hours before. He had felt proud and happy then, happy that she was his, proud of her grace and wifely carriage. But now, after the kindling again of so many memories, the first touch of her body, musical and strange and perfumed, sent through him a keen pang of lust. Under cover of her silence he

pressed her arm closely to his side; and, as they stood at
the hotel door, he felt that they had escaped from their
lives and duties, escaped from home and friends and
run away together with wild and radiant hearts to a new
adventure.

'The Dead', *Dubliners*

She asked me why I never came, said she had heard all sorts
of stories about me. This was only to gain time. Asked
me was I writing poems? About whom? I asked her. This
confused her more and I felt sorry and mean.

A Portrait of the Artist as a Young Man

... you cruel creature, little mite of a thing with a heart the
size of a fullstop.

Ulysses

Are you not weary of ardent ways ... Tell no more of
enchanted days.

A Portrait of the Artist as a Young Man

Her name sprang to my lips at moments in strange prayers
and praises which I myself did not understand. My eyes
were often full of tears (I could not tell why) and at times
a flood from my heart seemed to pour itself out into

my bosom. I thought little of the future. I did not know whether I would ever speak to her or not or, if I spoke to her, how I could tell her of my confused adoration. But my body was like a harp and her words and gestures were like fingers running upon the wires.

'Araby', *Dubliners*

And if he had judged her harshly? If her life were a simple rosary of hours, her life simple and strange as a bird's life, gay in the morning, restless all day, tired at sundown? Her heart simple and wilful as a bird's heart?

A Portrait of the Artist as a Young Man

Dear Henry

I got your last letter to me and thank you very much for it. I am sorry you did not like my last letter. Why did you enclose the stamps? I am awfully angry with you. I do wish I could punish you for that. I called you naughty boy because I do not like that other world. Please tell me what is the real meaning of that word. Are you not happy in your home you poor little naughty boy? I do wish I could do something for you. Please tell me what you think of poor me. I often think of the beautiful name you have. Dear Henry, when will we meet? I think of you so often you have no idea. I have never felt myself so much drawn

to a man as you. I feel so bad about. Please write me a
long letter and tell me more. Remember if you do not I
will punish you. So now you know what I will do to you,
you naughty boy, if you do not wrote. O how I long to
meet you. Henry dear, do not deny my request before my
patience are exhausted. Then I will tell you all. Goodbye
now, naughty darling, I have such a bad headache. today
and write *by return* to your longing

Martha.

P. S. Do tell me what kind of perfume does your wife
use. I want to know.

Ulysses

What's yours is mine and what's mine is my own.

Ulysses

It was cold autumn weather but in spite of the cold they
wandered up and down the roads of the Park for nearly
three hours. They agreed to break off their intercourse:
every bond, he said, is a bond to sorrow.

'A Painful Case' *Dubliners*

the sun shines for you he said the day we were lying among
the rhododendrons on Howth head in the grey tweed suit
and his straw hat the day I got him to propose to me yes

first I gave him the bit of seedcake out of my mouth and
it was leapyear like now yes 16 years ago my God after that
long kiss I near lost my breath yes he said I was a flower
of the mountain yes so we arc flowers all a womans body
yes that was one true thing he said in his life and the sun
shines for you today yes that was why I liked him because
I saw he understood or felt what a woman is and I knew I
could always get round him and I gave him all the pleasure
I could leading him on till he asked me to say yes and I
wouldnt answer first only looked out over the sea and the
sky I was thinking of so many things he didnt know
Ulysses

Love between man and man is impossible because there
must not be sexual intercourse and friendship between
man and woman is impossible because there must be sexual
intercourse.
'A Painful Case', *Dubliners*

He went often to her little cottage outside Dublin; often
they spent their evenings alone. Little by little, as their
thoughts entangled, they spoke of subjects less remote.
Her companionship was like a warm soil about an exotic.
Many times she allowed the dark to fall upon them,
refraining from lighting the lamp. The dark discreet

room, their isolation, the music that still vibrated in their ears united them. This union exalted him, wore away the rough edges of his character, emotionalised his mental life. Sometimes he caught himself listening to the sound of his own voice. He thought that in her eyes he would ascend to an angelical stature; and, as he attached the fervent nature of his companion more and more closely to him, he heard the strange impersonal voice which he recognised as his own, insisting on the soul's incurable loneliness. We cannot give ourselves, it said: we are our own.

'A Painful Case', *Dubliners*

… for she was the only girl they loved, as she is the queenly pearl you prize, because of the way the night that first we met she is bound to be, methinks, and not in vain, the darling of my heart, sleeping in her april cot, within her singachamer, with her greengageflavoured candywhistle duetted to the crazyquilt, Isobel, she is so pretty, truth to tell, wildwood's eyes and primarose hair, quietly, all the woods so wild, in mauves of moss and daphnedews, how all so still she lay, neath of the whitethorn, child of tree, like some losthappy leaf, like blowing flower stilled, as fain would she anon, for soon again 'twill be, win me, woo me, wed me, ah weary me!

Finnegans Wake

She would follow her dream of love, the dictates of her heart that told her he was her all in all, the only man in all the world for her for love was the master guide. Nothing else mattered. Come what might she would be wild, untrammelled, free.

Ulysses

I had never spoken to her, except for a few casual words, and yet her name was like a summons to all my foolish blood. Her image accompanied me even in places the most hostile to romance.

'Araby', *Dubliners*

She seemed to him so frail that he longed to defend her against something and then to be alone with her. Moments of their secret life together burst like stars upon his memory.

'The Dead', *Dubliners*

Yes, it was her he was looking at and there was meaning in his look. His eyes burned into her as though they would search her through and through, read her very soul.

Ulysses

A girl stood before him in midstream, alone and still, gazing out to sea. She seemed like one whom magic had changed into the likeness of a strange and beautiful seabird. Her long slender bare legs were delicate as a crane's and pure save where an emerald trail of seaweed had fashioned itself as a sign upon the flesh. Her thighs, fuller and soft-hued as ivory, were bared almost to the hips, where the white fringes of her drawers were like feathering of soft white down. Her slate-blue skirts were kilted boldly about her waist and dovetailed behind her. Her bosom was as a bird's, soft and slight, slight and soft as the breast of some dark-plumaged dove. But her long fair hair was girlish: and girlish, and touched with the wonder of mortal beauty, her face.

She was alone and still, gazing out to sea; and when she felt his presence and the worship of his eyes her eyes turned to him in quiet sufferance of his gaze, without shame or wantonness. Long, long she suffered his gaze and then quietly withdrew her eyes from his and bent them towards the stream, gently stirring the water with her foot hither and thither. The first faint noise of gently moving water broke the silence, low and faint and whispering, faint as the bells of sleep; hither and thither, hither and thither; and a faint flame trembled on her cheek.

—Heavenly God! cried Stephen's soul, in an outburst of profane joy.

He turned away from her suddenly and set off across the strand. His cheeks were aflame; his body was aglow; his limbs were trembling. On and on and on and on he strode, far out over the sands, singing wildly to the sea, crying to greet the advent of the life that had cried to him. Her image had passed into his soul for ever and no word had broken the holy silence of his ecstasy. Her eyes had called him and his soul had leaped at the call. To live, to err, to fall, to triumph, to recreate life out of life! A wild angel had appeared to him, the angel of mortal youth and beauty, an envoy from the fair courts of life, to throw open before him in an instant of ecstasy the gates of all the ways of error and glory. On and on and on and on!

A Portrait of the Artist as a Young Man

A cloud began to cover the sun slowly, wholly, shadowing the bay in deeper green. It lay beneath him, a bowl of bitter waters. Fergus' song: I sang it above in the house, holding down the long dark chords. Her door was open: she wanted to hear my music. Silent with awe and pity I went to her bedside. She was crying in her wretched bed. For those words, Stephen: love's bitter mystery.

Ulysses

When he gained the crest of the Magazine Hill he halted and looked along the river towards Dublin, the lights of which burned redly and hospitably in the cold night. He looked down the slope and, at the base, in the shadow of the wall of the Park, he saw some human figures lying. Those venal and furtive loves filled him with despair. He gnawed the rectitude of his life; he felt that he had been outcast from life's feast. One human being had seemed to love him and he had denied her life and happiness: he had sentenced her to ignominy, a death of shame. He knew that the prostrate creatures down by the wall were watching him and wished him gone. No one wanted him; he was outcast from life's feast.

'A Painful Case', *Dubliners*

They used to drive a stake of wood through his heart in the grave. As if it wasn't broken already.

Ulysses

Why cant you kiss a man without going and marrying him first you sometimes love to wildly when you feel that way so nice all over you you cant help yourself I wish some man or other would take me sometime when hes there and kiss me in his arms theres nothing like a kiss long and hot down to your soul almost paralyses you

Ulysses

I was a Flower of the mountain yes when I put the rose in my hair like the Andalusian girls used or shall I wear a red yes and how he kissed me under the Moorish wall and I thought well as well him as another ... then he asked me would I yes to say yes my mountain flower and first I put my arms around him yes and drew him down to me so he could feel my breasts all perfume yes and his heart was going like mad and yes I said yes I will Yes.

Ulysses

Wind whines and whines the shingle,
The crazy pierstakes groan;
A senile sea numbers each single
Slimesilvered stone.

From whining wind and colder
Grey sea I wrap him warm
And touch his trembling fineboned shoulder
And boyish arm.

Around us fear, descending
Darkness of fear above
And in my heart how deep unending
Ache of love!

'On the Beach at Fontana', from *Pomes Penyeach*

My love is in a light attire
  Among the apple-trees,
Where the gay winds do most desire
  To run in companies.

There, where the gay winds stay to woo
  The young leaves as they pass,
My love goes slowly, bending to
  Her shadow on the grass;

And where the sky's a pale blue cup
  Over the laughing land,
My love goes lightly, holding up
  Her dress with dainty hand.
'VII', from *Chamber Music*

A Young Man

a Young Man

felt his belly crave for its food. He hoped th
Mulligan came from the stairhead

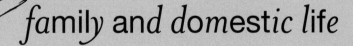

family and *domestic life*

Stately, plump Buck Mulligan came from the stairhead, bearing a bowl of lather on which a mirror and a razor lay crossed. A yellow dressinggown, ungirdled, was sustained gently behind him by the mild morning air.

Ulysses

—Whatever else is unsure in this stinking dunghill of a world a mother's love is not. Your mother brings you into the world, carries you first in her body. What do we know about what she feels? But whatever she feels, it, at least, must be real. It must be. What are our ideas or ambitions? Play. Ideas! Why ... Every jackass going the roads thinks he has ideas.

A Portrait of the Artist as a Young Man

"we really are all hungry and when we are hungry we are all very quarrelsome."

'The Dead', *Dubliners*

What is home without Plumtree's Potted Meat? Incomplete.

Ulysses

She respected her husband in the same way as she respected the General Post Office, as something large, secure and fixed; and though she knew the small number of his talents, she appreciated his abstract value as a male. 'A Mother', *Dubliners*

What lay under exposure on the lower, middle and upper shelves of the kitchen dresser, opened by Bloom?

On the lower shelf five vertical breakfast plates, six horizontal breakfast saucers on which rested inverted breakfast cups, a moustachecup, uninverted, and saucer of Crown Derby, four white goldrimmed eggcups, an open shammy purse displaying coins, mostly copper, and a phial of aromatic (violet) comfits. On the middle shelf a chipped eggcup containing pepper, a drum of table salt, four conglomerated black olives in oleaginous paper, an empty pot of Plumtree's potted meat, an oval wicker basket bedded with fibre and containing one Jersey pear, a halfempty bottle of William Gilbey and Co's white invalid port, half disrobed of its swathe of coralpink tissue paper, a packet of Epps's soluble cocoa, five ounces of Anne Lynch's choice tea at 2/— per lb in a crinkled leadpaper bag, a cylindrical canister containing the best crystallised lump sugar, two onions, one, the larger, Spanish, entire, the other, smaller, Irish, bisected with augmented surface and more redolent, a jar of Irish Model Dairy's cream, a jug of brown crockery containing a naggin and a quarter of soured adulterated milk, converted by heat into water, acidulous serum and semisolidified curds, which added to the quantity subtracted for Mr Bloom's and Mrs Fleming's breakfasts, made one imperial pint, the total quantity originally delivered, two cloves, a halfpenny and a small dish containing a slice of fresh ribsteak. On the upper shelf a battery of jamjars (empty) of various sizes and proveniences.

Ulysses

He ate his dinner with surly appetite and when the meal was over and the grease-strewn plates lay abandoned on the table, he rose and went to the window, clearing the thick scum from his mouth with his tongue and licking it from his lips. So he had sunk to the state of a beast that licks his chaps after meat.

A Portrait of the Artist as a Young Man

The light music of whiskey falling into glasses made an agreeable interlude.

'Grace', *Dubliners*

Don't eat a beefsteak. If you do the eyes of that cow will pursue you through all eternity.

Ulysses

Mr Leopold Bloom ate with relish the inner organs of beasts and fowls. He liked thick giblet soup, nutty gizzards, a stuffed roast heart, liverslices fried with crustcrumbs, fried hencods' roes. Most of all he liked grilled mutton kidneys which gave to his palate a fine tang of faintly scented urine.

Ulysses

The swift December dusk had come tumbling clownishly after its dull day and, as he stared through the dull square of the window of the schoolroom, he felt his belly crave for its food. He hoped there would be stew for dinner, turnips and carrots and bruised potatoes and fat mutton pieces to be ladled out in thick peppered flour-fattened sauce. Stuff it into you, his belly counselled him.

A Portrait of the Artist as a Young Man

A father, Stephen said, battling against hopelessness, is a necessary evil.

Ulysses

Paternity may be a legal fiction. Who is the father of any son that any son should love him or he any son?

Ulysses

The son unborn mars beauty: born, he brings pain,
divides affection, increases care. He is a male: his growth
is his father's decline, his youth his father's envy, his friend
his father's enemy.

Ulysses

Frail the white rose and frail are
Her hands that gave
Whose soul is sere and paler
Than time's wan wave.

Rosefrail and fair – yet frailest
A wonder wild
In gentle eyes thou veilest,
My blueveined child.

'A Flower Given to My Daughter', from *Pomes Penyeach*

—Mkgnao!
—O, there you are, Mr Bloom said, turning from the fire.

The cat mewed in answer and stalked again stiffly round
a leg of the table, mewing. Just how she stalks over my
writingtable. Prr. Scratch my head. Prr.

Mr Bloom watched curiously, kindly, the lithe black
form. Clean to see: the gloss of her sleek hide, the white

button under the butt of her tail, the green flashing eyes. He bent down to her, his hands on his knees.

—Milk for the pussens, he said.

—Mrkgnao! the cat cried.

They call them stupid. They understand what we say better than we understand them. She understands all she wants to. Vindictive too. Wonder what I look like to her. Height of a tower? No, she can jump me.

—Afraid of the chickens she is, he said mockingly. Afraid of the chookchooks. I never saw such a stupid pussens as the pussens.

Cruel. Her nature. Curious mice never squeal. Seem to like it.

—Mrkrgnao! the cat said loudly.

She blinked up out of her avid shameclosing eyes, mewing plaintively and long, showing him her milkwhite teeth. He watched the dark eyeslits narrowing with greed till her eyes were green stones. Then he went to the dresser took the jug Hanlon's milkman had just filled for him, poured warmbubbled milk on a saucer and set it slowly on the floor.

—Gurrhr! she cried, running to lap.

Ulysses

Though their life was modest, they believed in eating well;
the best of everything: diamond-bone sirloins, three-
shilling tea and the best bottled stout.

'The Dead', *Dubliners*

Haines sat down to pour out the tea.

—I'm giving you two lumps each, he said. But, I say,
Mulligan, you do make strong tea, don't you?

Buck Mulligan, hewing thick slices from the loaf, said in
an old woman's wheedling voice:

—When I makes tea I makes tea, as old mother Grogan
said. And when I makes water I makes water.

Ulysses

Once upon a time and a very good time it was there was
a moocow coming down along the road and this moocow
that was coming down along the road met a nicens little
boy named baby tuckoo

His father told him that story: his father looked at him
through a glass: he had a hairy face.

He was baby tuckoo. The moocow came down the road
where Betty Byrne lived: she sold lemon platt.

 O, the wild rose blossoms

 On the little green place.

He sang that song. That was his song.

O, the green wothe botheth.

When you wet the bed first it is warm then it gets cold.
His mother put on the oilsheet. That had the queer smell.

His mother had a nicer smell than his father. She played
on the piano the sailor's hornpipe for him to dance. He
danced:

Tralala lala, Tralala tralaladdy, Tralala lala, Tralala lala.

A Portrait of the Artist as a Young Man

He could not make up his mind whether to like her or
despise her for what she had done. Of course he had done
it too. His instinct urged him to remain free, not to marry.
Once you are married you are done for, it said.

'The Boarding House', *Dubliners*

So she had had that romance in her life: a man had died
for her sake. It hardly pained him now to think how poor
a part he, her husband, had played in her life. He watched
her while she slept, as though he and she had never lived
together as man and wife.

'The Dead', *Dubliners*

A corpse is meat gone bad. Well and what's cheese? Corpse
of milk.

Ulysses

art, literature and *music*

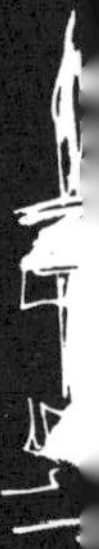

"[A writer ...

For that (the rapt one ...

with the acquaintance of ...

over to carry three score and ten toptypsical reading ...

would sunder) till Daleth, mahomahouma, who ope...

Finnegans Wake

bread of experience int...

life." *A Portrait of the Ar...*

To spea...

unders...

again, ...

colour ...

come t...

A Portr...

hides and hints and misses in pi . . ill ye finally (through not yet endlike

ation, transmuting the d ly

little typtopies. Fill up. So you need hardly sp . . . ow every word will

the book of Doublends Jined (may his forehead be darkened with mud

radiant body of everliving

ereor the Do

at beauty which ' es to expres

a *Young Man* ver of his soul,

of the Artist a

thing, new and so le, imperishable

wly and humbly and cons

arth or what it brings fort'

son gates of our soul, ar

hat is art.

s *a Young Man* nps of earth

ificer whose name he bore, a

e *Artist as a Young Man*

What is that beauty which the artist struggles to express
from lumps of earth

A Portrait of the Artist as a Young Man

As the poet says: *Great minds are very near to madness*
'**Grace**', *Dubliners*

He would create proudly out of the freedom and power
of his soul, as the great artificer whose name he bore, a
living thing, new and soaring and beautiful, impalpable,
imperishable.

A Portrait of the Artist as a Young Man

'Tis as human a little story as paper could well carry

Finnegans Wake

To speak of these things and to try to understand their
nature and, having understood it, to try slowly and humbly
and constantly to express, to press out again, from the
gross earth or what it brings forth, from sound and shape
and colour which are the prison gates of our soul, an
image of the beauty we have come to understand
— that is art.

A Portrait of the Artist as a Young Man

For that (the rapt one warns) is what papyr is meed of, made of, hides and hints and misses in prints. Till ye finally (though not yet endlike) meet with the acquaintance of Mister Typus, Mistress Tope and all the little typtopies. Fillstup. So you need hardly spell me how every word will be bound over to carry three score and ten toptypsical readings throughout the book of Doublends Jined (may his forehead be darkened with mud who would sunder!) till Daleth, mahomahouma, who oped it closeth thereof the. Dor.

Finnegans Wake

Mother indulgent. Said I have a queer mind and have read too much. Not true. Have read little and understood less.

A Portrait of the Artist as a Young Man

You know Manningham's story of the burgher's wife who bade Dick Burbage to her bed after she had seen him in *Richard III* and how Shakespeare, overhearing, without more ado about nothing, took the cow by the horns and, when Burbage came knocking at the gate, answered from the capon's blankets: *William the conqueror came before Richard III*.

Ulysses

The object of any work of art is the transference of
emotion; talent is the gift of conveying that emotion.
From *Conversations with James Joyce* by Arthur Power

"[A writer is] a priest of the eternal imagination,
transmuting the daily bread of experience into the radiant
body of everliving life."
A Portrait of the Artist as a Young Man

Suck was a queer word … the sound was ugly. Once he had
washed his hands in the lavatory of the Wicklow Hotel and
his father pulled the stopper up by the chain after and the
dirty water went down through the hole in the basin. And
when it had all gone down slowly the hole in the basin had
made a sound like that: suck. Only louder.
A Portrait of the Artist as a Young Man

—When may we expect to have something from you on the
esthetic question? he asked.
—From me! said Stephen in astonishment. I stumble on an
idea once a fortnight if I am lucky.
—These questions are very profound, Mr Dedalus, said the
dean. It is like looking down from the cliffs of Moher into
the depths. Many go down into the depths and never come
up. Only the trained diver can go down into those depths

and explore them and come to the surface again.

A Portrait of the Artist as a Young Man

—I'm an emotional man, said Temple. That's quite rightly expressed. And I'm proud that I'm an emotionalist.

A Portrait of the Artist as a Young Man

Bosh! Stephen said rudely. A man of genius makes no mistakes. His errors are volitional and are the portals of discovery.

Ulysses

Plato, I believe, said that beauty is the splendour of truth. I don't think that it has a meaning, but the true and the beautiful are akin.

A Portrait of the Artist as a Young Man

The demand that I make of my reader is that he should devote his whole life to reading my works.
James Joyce Interview with Max Eastman in *Harper's Magazine*, as quoted in *James Joyce* (1959) by Richard Ellmann.

The object of the artist is the creation of the beautiful. What the beautiful is is another question.

A Portrait of the Artist as a Young Man

I've put in so many enigmas and puzzles that it will
keep the professors busy for centuries arguing over
what I meant, and that's the only way of insuring one's
immortality.

James Joyce on *Ulysses*, from Richard Ellmann's *James Joyce*,
Oxford University Press, New York, Revised Edition
(1982)

A light began to tremble on the horizon of his mind.
He was not so old — thirty-two. His temperament might
be said to be just at the point of maturity. There were so
many different moods and impressions that he wished
to express in verse. He felt them within him. He tried to
weigh his soul to see if it was a poet's soul. Melancholy was
the dominant note of his temperament, he thought, but
it was a melancholy tempered by recurrences of faith and
resignation and simple joy.

'A Little Cloud', *Dubliners*

Art thou pale for weariness
Of climbing heaven and gazing on the earth,
Wandering companionless… ?'

He repeated to himself the lines of Shelley's fragment.
Its alternation of sad human ineffectiveness with vast
inhuman cycles of activity chilled him and he forgot his

own human and ineffectual grieving.

A Portrait of the Artist as a Young Man

To discover the mode of life or of art whereby your spirit could express itself in unfettered freedom.

A Portrait of the Artist as a Young Man

He stood still in the gloom of the hall, trying to catch the air that the voice was singing and gazing up at his wife. There was grace and mystery in her attitude as if she were a symbol of something. He asked himself what is a woman standing on the stairs in the shadow, listening to distant music, a symbol of. If he were a painter he would paint her in that attitude. Her blue felt hat would show off the bronze of her hair against the darkness and the dark panels of her skirt would show off the light ones. *Distant Music* he would call the picture if he were a painter.

'The Dead', *Dubliners*

I enquired about Ulysses. Was it progressing?

"I have been working hard on it all day," said Joyce.

"Does that mean that you have written a great deal?" I said.

"Two sentences," said Joyce.

I looked sideways but Joyce was not smiling. I thought of Flaubert.

"You have been seeking the *mot juste*?" I said.

"No," said Joyce. "I have the words already. What I am seeking is the perfect order of words in the sentence."

Frank Budgen, *James Joyce and the Making of Ulysses* (1934)

The artist, like the God of creation, remains within or behind or beyond or above his handiwork, invisible, refined out of existence, indifferent, paring his fingernails.

A Portrait of the Artist as a Young Man

Art has to reveal to us ideas, formless spiritual essences. The supreme question about a work of art is out of how deep a life does it spring.

Ulysses

A tremor passed over his body. How sad and how beautiful! He wanted to cry quietly but not for himself: for the words, so beautiful and sad, like music.

A Portrait of the Artist as a Young Man

Shakespeare is the happy hunting ground of all minds that have lost their balance.

Ulysses

Numbers it is. All music when you come to think …
Musemathematics. And you think you're listening to the
etherial.

Ulysses

Any object, intensely regarded, may be a gate of access to
the incorruptible eon of the gods.

Ulysses

The music passed in an instant, as the first bars of sudden
music always did, over the fantastic fabrics of his mind,
dissolving them painlessly and noiselessly as a sudden wave
dissolves the sand-built turrets of children.

A Portrait of the Artist as a Young Man

He found something mean in the pretty furniture which
he had bought for his house on the hire system. Annie had
chosen it herself and it reminded him of her. It too was
prim and pretty. A dull resentment against his life awoke
within him. Could he not escape from his little house?
Was it too late for him to try to live bravely like Gallaher?
Could he go to London? There was the furniture still to be
paid for. If he could only write a book and get it published,
that might open the way for him.

'A Little Cloud', *Dubliners*

There is an art in lighting a fire. We have the liberal arts and we have the useful arts. This is one of the useful arts.

A Portrait of the Artist as a Young Man

For that (the rapt one warns) is what papyr is meed of, made of, hides and hints and misses in prints.

Finnegans Wake

—It is a symbol of Irish art. The cracked lookingglass of a servant.

Ulysses

You have asked me what I would do and what I would not do. I will tell you what I will do and what I will not do. I will not serve that in which I no longer believe, whether it call itself my home, my fatherland, or my church: and I will try to express myself in some mode of life or art as freely as I can and as wholly as I can, using for my defence the only arms I allow myself to use—silence, exile, and cunning.

A Portrait of the Artist as a Young Man

Ladies and gents, you are here assembled

To hear why earth and heaven trembled

Because of the black and sinister arts

Of an Irish writer in foreign parts.

…

I'll burn that book, so help me devil.

I'll sing a psalm as I watch it burn

And the ashes I'll keep in a one-handled urn.

I'll penance do with farts and groans

Kneeling upon my marrowbones.

This very next lent I will unbare

My penitent buttocks to the air

And sobbing beside my printing press

My awful sin I will confess.

My Irish foreman from Bannockburn

Shall dip his right hand in the urn

And sign crisscross with reverent thumb

Memento homo upon my bum.

Lines from '*Gas from a Burner*'

magination he beheld ...s w... ...s and saw ag
...ries and saw again the leer of the yo ng ... ...spirit. He w
...and spirit. He was tired of knocking about... of ...November. Would he ...to
November. Would he ...2 W...
...ld be to have a warm fire to sit by and a good dinner ...to sit down again...
I began to hunger again for wild sensations, for the escape which tho...
...and with girls. He kne...
...myself. But real adven...
...waves rushing there...
'An Encounter', *Dubliners*
...heart good to see the rivers...
Gallants', *Dubliners*
...heart good to a... rivers and lake... a...
...as for them saying theres n... God I wou...t giv... ...ap of my tw... je...

yours

of money and

'Li ...'

living

said, I wish you had

you had, I wish you

around

day,

you

I began to hunger again for wild sensations, for the escape
which those chronicles of disorder alone seemed to offer
me ... I wanted real adventures to happen to myself. But
real adventures, I reflected, do not happen to people who
remain at home: they must be sought abroad.
'An Encounter', *Dubliners*

But all they are all there scraping along to sneeze out a
likelihood that will solve and salve life's robulous rebus
Finnegans Wake

He lived at a little distance from his body, regarding
his own acts with doubtful side-glances. He had an odd
autobiographical habit which led him to compose in his
mind from time to time a short sentence about himself
containing a subject in the third person and a predicate in
the past tense.
'A Painful Case', *Dubliners*

A Place for Every-thing and Everything in its Place, Is the
Pen Mightier than the Sword? A Successful Career in the
Civil Service
Finnegans Wake

I could not call my wandering thoughts together. I had hardly any patience with the serious work of life which, now that it stood between me and my desire, seemed to me child's play, ugly monotonous child's play.

'Araby', *Dubliners*

In his imagination he beheld the pair of lovers walking along some dark road; he heard Corley's voice in deep energetic gallantries and saw again the leer of the young woman's mouth. This vision made him feel keenly his own poverty of purse and spirit. He was tired of knocking about, of pulling the devil by the tail, of shifts and intrigues. He would be thirty-one in November. Would he never get a good job? Would he never have a home of his own? He thought how pleasant it would be to have a warm fire to sit by and a good dinner to sit down to. He had walked the streets long enough with friends and with girls. He knew what those friends were worth: he knew the girls too. Experience had embittered his heart against the world. But all hope had not left him. He felt better after having eaten than he had felt before, less weary of his life, less vanquished in spirit. He might yet be able to settle down in some snug corner and live happily

'Two Gallants', *Dubliners*

"Well, Tommy," he said, "I wish you and yours every joy in life, old chap, and tons of money, and may you never die till I shoot you.

'A Little Cloud', *Dubliners*

Why was he doubly irritated?

Because he had forgotten and because he remembered that he had reminded himself twice not to forget.

Ulysses

Think you're escaping and run into yourself. Longest way round is the shortest way home.

Ulysses

Mother is putting my new secondhand clothes in order. She prays now, she says, that I may learn in my own life and away from home and friends what the heart is and what it feels. Amen. So be it. Welcome, O life, I go to encounter for the millionth time the reality of experience and to forge in the smithy of my soul the uncreated conscience of my race.

A Portrait of the Artist as a Young Man

... yet it wounded him to think that he would never be but a shy guest at the feast of the world's culture

A Portrait of the Artist as a Young Man

How mingled and imperfect are all our sublunary joys.

Ulysses

The barometer of his emotional nature was set for a spell of riot.

'Counterparts', *Dubliners*

Death is the highest form of life.

Ulysses

Rarely smoke, dear. Cigar now and then. Childish device. *(Lewdly.)* The mouth can be better engaged than with a cylinder of rank weed.

Ulysses

> —If anyone thinks that I amn't divine
> He'll get no free drinks when I'm making the wine
> But have to drink water and wish it were plain
> That I make when the wine becomes water again.

Ulysses

Alone, what did Bloom feel?

The cold of interstellar space, thousands of degrees below freezing point or the absolute zero of Fahrenheit, Centigrade or Réaumur: the incipient intimations of proximate dawn.

Ulysses

The Gracehoper was always jigging ajog, hoppy on akkant of his joyicity ...

Finnegans Wake

It was hard work – a hard life – but now that she was about to leave it she did not find it a wholly undesirable life.

'Eveline', *Dubliners*

While you have a thing it can be taken from you ... ... But when you give it, you have given it. No robber can take it from you. [He bends his head and presses his son's hand against his cheek.] It is yours then for ever when you have given it. It will be yours always. That is to give.

Exiles

All moanday, tearsday, wailsday, thumpsday, frightday, shatterday ...

Finnegans Wake

If Socrates leave his house today he will find the sage seated on his doorstep, If Judas go forth tonight it is to Judas his steps will tend. Every life is many days, day after day. We walk through ourselves, meeting robbers, ghosts, giants, old men, young men, wives, widows, brothers-in-love, but always meeting ourselves.

Ulysses

What's in a name? That is what we ask ourselves in childhood when we write the name that we are told is ours.

Ulysses

To learn one must be humble. But life is the great teacher.

Ulysses

Ah, there's no friends like the old friends," she said ...

'The Sisters', *Dubliners*

First we feel. Then we fall.

Finnegans Wake

But he was not sick there. He thought that he was sick in his heart if you could be sick in that place.

A Portrait of the Artist as a Young Man

Begin to forget it. It will remember itself from every
sides, with all gestures, in each our word. Today's truth,
tomorrow's trend.

Finnegans Wake

I love flowers Id love to have the whole place swimming
in roses God of heaven theres nothing like nature the
wild mountains then the sea and the waves rushing then
the beautiful country with fields of oats and wheat and
all kinds of things and all the fine cattle going about that
would do your heart good to see rivers and lakes and
flowers all sorts of shapes and smells and colours springing
up even out of the ditches primroses and violets nature it
is as for them saying theres no God I wouldnt give a snap
of my two fingers for all their learning

Ulysses

The peace of the gardens and the kindly lights in the
windows poured a tender influence into his restless heart.

A Portrait of the Artist as a Young Man

I smiled at him. *America,* I said, quietly, just like that. *What
is it? The sweepings of every country including our own. Isn't that true?*
That's a fact.

Ulysses

He travels after a winter sun,
Urging the cattle along a cold red road,
Calling to them, a voice they know,
He drives his beasts above Cabra.

The voice tells them home is warm.
They moo and make brute music with their hoofs.
He drives them with a flowering branch before him,
Smoke pluming their foreheads.

Boor, bond of the herd,
Tonight stretch full by the fire!
I bleed by the black stream
For my torn bough!
'Tilly', from *Pomes Penyeach*

He went up to his room after dinner in order to be alone
with his soul, and at every step his soul seemed to sigh; at
every step his soul mounted with his feet, sighing in the
ascent, through a region of viscid gloom.

A Portrait of the Artist as a Young Man

Staunch friend, a brother soul: Wilde's love that dare not speak its name. His arm; Cranly's arm. He now will leave me. And the blame? As I am. As I am. All or not at all.
Ulysses

Life, he himself said once, (his biografiend, in fact, kills him verysoon, if yet not, after) is a wake, livit or krikit, and on the bunk of our bread-winning lies the cropse of our seedfather, a phrase which the establisher of the world by law might pretinately write across the chestfront of all manorwombanborn.
Finnegans Wake

—Because you don't save, Mr Deasy said, pointing his finger. You don't know yet what money is. Money is power. When you have lived as long as I have. I know, I know. If youth but knew. But what does Shakespeare say? *Put but money in thy purse.*
Ulysses

His line of life had not been the shortest distance between two points and for short periods he had been driven to live by his wits.
'Grace', *Dubliners*

You die for your country. Suppose. *(He places his arm on Private Carr's sleeve)* Not that I wish it for you. But I say: Let my country die for me. Up to the present it has done so. I don't want it to die. Damn death. Long live life!

Ulysses

Gabriel's warm trembling fingers tapped the cold pane of the window. How cool it must be outside! How pleasant it would be to walk out alone, first along by the river and then through the park! The snow would be lying on the branches of the trees and forming a bright cap on the top of the Wellington Monument. How much more pleasant it would be there than at the supper-table!

'The Dead', *Dubliners*

Never back a woman you defend, never get quit of a friend on whom you depend never make face to a foe till he's rife and never get stuck to another man's pfife.

Finnegans Wake

The adventure of meeting Gallaher after eight years, of finding himself with Gallaher in Corless's surrounded by lights and noise, of listening to Gallaher's stories and of sharing for a brief space Gallaher's vagrant and triumphant life, upset the equipoise of his sensitive nature. He felt

acutely the contrast between his own life and his friend's
and it seemed to him unjust. Gallaher was his inferior
in birth and education. He was sure that he could do
something better than his friend had ever done, or could
ever do, something higher than mere tawdry journalism if
he only got the chance. What was it that stood in his way?
His unfortunate timidity! He wished to vindicate himself
in some way, to assert his manhood.

'A Little Cloud', *Dubliners*

I resent violence or intolerance in any shape or form. It
never reaches anything or stops anything. A revolution
must come on the due instalments plan. It's a patent
absurdity on the face of it to hate people because they live
round the corner and speak another vernacular, so to
speak.

Ulysses

desire and *sex*

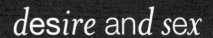

shapely goddesses, Venus, Juno: curves the world admires,

woman dressed in a long pink gown laid her hand on his arm to detain

...ere trembling with

...accord! To take her as she was...

...old, the wild...

...urges us to aba...

Beauty...bicky backy beauty, shapely...

...arms held him...dressed her face lifted to...

...arrested

— Redheaded

Ulysses

...is it was too much for him. He cl...

...broke the peace of the night save...

...upon his brain as upon his lips as t...

...forgetting to go...odour.

Portrait of the Artist as a

Beauty: it curves: curves are beauty. Shapely goddesses, Venus, Juno: curves the world admires.

Ulysses

He kissed the plump mellow yellow smellow melons of her rump, on each plump melonous hemisphere, in their mellow yellow furrow, with obscure prolonged provocative melonsmellonous osculation.

Ulysses

If she would only turn to him or come to him of her own accord! To take her as she was would be brutal. No, he must see some ardour in her eyes first. He longed to be master of her strange mood.

'The Dead', *Dubliners*

I suppose she was pious because no man would look at her twice

Ulysses

He foresaw his pale body reclined in it at full, naked, in a womb of warmth, oiled by scented melting soap, softly laved. He saw his trunk and limbs riprippled over and sustained, buoyed lightly upward, lemonyellow: his navel, bud of flesh: and saw the dark tangled curls of his bush floating, floating hair of the stream around the limp father of thousands, a languid floating flower.

Ulysses

Here, and it goes on to appear now, she comes, a peacefugle, a parody's bird, a peri potmother, a pringlpik in the ilandiskippy, with peewee and powwows in beggybaggy on her bickybacky and a flick flask fleckflinging its pixylighting pacts' huemeramybows, picking here, pecking there, pussypussy plunderpussy.

Finnegans Wake

She would follow, her dream of love, the dictates of her heart that told her he was her all in all, the only man in all the world for her for love was the master guide. Nothing else mattered. Come what might she would be wild, untrammelled, free.

Ulysses

He could have flung his arms about her hips and held her still, for his arms were trembling with desire to seize her and only the stress of his nails against the palms of his hands held the wild impulse of his body in check.

'The Dead', *Dubliners*

You bore me away, framed me in oak and tinsel, set me above your marriage couch. Unseen, one summer eve, you kissed me in four places. And with loving pencil you shaded my eyes, my bosom and my shame.

Ulysses

—Do you know why those fellows scut? I will tell you but you must not let on you know.

—Tell us, Athy. Go on. You might if you know.

He paused for a moment and then said mysteriously:

—They were caught with Simon Moonan and Tusker Boyle in the square one night.

The fellows looked at him and asked:

—Caught?

—What doing?

Athy said:

—Smugging.

A Portrait of the Artist as a Young Man

Our flesh shrinks from what it dreads and responds to the stimulus of what it desires by a purely reflex action of the nervous system. Our eyelid closes before we are aware that the fly is about to enter our eye.

A Portrait of the Artist as a Young Man

He stood still in the middle of the roadway, his heart clamouring against his bosom in a tumult. A young woman dressed in a long pink gown laid her hand on his arm to detain him and gazed into his face. She said gaily:

—Good night, Willie dear!

Her room was warm and lightsome. A huge doll sat with her legs apart in the copious easy-chair beside the bed. He tried to bid his tongue speak that he might seem at ease, watching her as she undid her gown, noting the proud conscious movements of her perfumed head.

As he stood silent in the middle of the room she came over to him and embraced him gaily and gravely. Her round arms held him firmly to her and he, seeing her face lifted to him in serious calm and feeling the warm calm rise and fall of her breast, all but burst into hysterical weeping. Tears of joy and relief shone in his delighted eyes and his lips parted though they would not speak.

She passed her tinkling hand through his hair, calling him a little rascal.

—Give me a kiss, she said.

His lips would not bend to kiss her. He wanted to be held firmly in her arms, to be caressed slowly, slowly, slowly. In her arms he felt that he had suddenly become strong and fearless and sure of himself. But his lips would not bend to kiss her.

With a sudden movement she bowed his head and joined her lips to his and he read the meaning of her movements in her frank uplifted eyes. It was too much for him. He closed his eyes, surrendering himself to her, body and mind, conscious of nothing in the world but the dark pressure of her softly parting lips. They pressed upon his brain as upon his lips as though they were the vehicle of a vague speech; and between them he felt an unknown and timid pressure, darker than the swoon of sin, softer than sound or odour.

A Portrait of the Artist as a Young Man

—Pascal, if I remember rightly, would not suffer his mother to kiss him as he feared the contact of her sex.

A Portrait of the Artist as a Young Man

For him there was nothing amusing in a girl's interest and regard. All day he had thought of nothing but their leave-taking on the steps of the tram at Harold's Cross, the stream of moody emotions it had made to course through him and the poem he had written about it. All day he had imagined a new meeting with her for he knew that she was to come to the play.

A Portrait of the Artist as a Young Man

Bite my laughters, drink my tears. Pore into me, volumes, spell me stark and spill me swooning. I just don't care what my thwarters think. Transname me loveliness, now and here me for all times!

Finnegans Wake

They would meet quietly as if they had known each other and had made their tryst, perhaps at one of the gates or in some more secret place. They would be alone, surrounded by darkness and silence: and in that moment of supreme tenderness he would be transfigured.

He would fade into something impalpable under her eyes and then in a moment he would be transfigured. Weakness and timidity and inexperience would fall from him in that magic moment.

A Portrait of the Artist as a Young Man

Desire urges us to possess, to go to something; loathing urges us to abandon, to go from something. The arts which excite them, pornographical or didactic, are therefore improper arts. The esthetic emotion (I used the general term) is therefore static. The mind is arrested and raised above desire and loathing.

A Portrait of the Artist as a Young Man

Even if we are often led to desire through the sense of beauty can you say that the beautiful is what we desire?

Exiles

His heart was brimming over with happiness. Just when he was wishing for it she had come to him of her own accord. Perhaps her thoughts had been running with his. Perhaps she had felt the impetuous desire that was in him, and then the yielding mood had come upon her.

'The Dead', *Dubliners*

Weary! Weary! He too was weary of ardent ways.

A Portrait of the Artist as a Young Man

A glow of desire kindled again his soul and fired and fulfilled all his body. Conscious of his desire she was waking from odorous sleep, the temptress of his villanelle. Her eyes, dark and with a look of languor, were opening to his eyes. Her nakedness yielded to him, radiant, warm, odorous and lavish-limbed, enfolded him like a shining cloud, enfolded him like water with a liquid life; and like a cloud of vapour or like waters circumfluent in space the liquid letters of speech, symbols of the element of mystery, flowed forth over his brain.

A Portrait of the Artist as a Young Man

She had thrown a shawl about her and, as they went together towards the tram, sprays of her fresh warm breath flew gaily above her cowled head and her shoes tapped blithely on the glassy road.

It was the last tram. The lank brown horses knew it and shook their bells to the clear night in admonition. The conductor talked with the driver, both nodding often in the green light of the lamp. On the empty seats of the tram were scattered a few coloured tickets. No sound of footsteps came up or down the road. No sound broke the peace of the night save when the lank brown horses rubbed their noses together and shook their bells.

They seemed to listen, he on the upper step and she on the lower. She came up to his step many times and went down to hers again between their phrases and once or twice stood close beside him for some moments on the upper step, forgetting to go down, and then went down. His heart danced upon her movements like a cork upon a tide. He heard what her eyes said to him from beneath their cowl and knew that in some dim past, whether in life or revery, he had heard their tale before. He saw her urge her vanities, her fine dress and sash and long black stockings, and knew that he had yielded to them a thousand times. Yet a voice within him spoke above the noise of his dancing heart, asking him would he take her gift to which he

had only to stretch out his hand. And he remembered
the day when he and Eileen had stood looking into the
hotel grounds, watching the waiters running up a trail of
bunting on the flagstaff and the fox terrier scampering
to and fro on the sunny lawn and how, all of a sudden,
she had broken out into a peal of laughter and had run
down the sloping curve of the path. Now, as then, he stood
listlessly in his place, seemingly a tranquil watcher of the
scene before him.

—She too wants me to catch hold of her, he thought. That's
why she came with me to the tram. I could easily catch hold
of her when she comes up to my step: nobody is looking. I
could hold her and kiss her.

But he did neither: and, when he was sitting alone in
the deserted tram, he tore his ticket into shreds and stared
gloomily at the corrugated footboard.

A Portrait of the Artist as a Young Man

—Redheaded women buck like goats.

Ulysses

O Sweetheart, hear you
  Your lover's tale;
A man shall have sorrow
  When friends him fail.

For he shall know then
  Friends be untrue
And a little ashes
  Their words come to.

But one unto him
  Will softly move
And softly woo him
  In ways of love.

His hand is under
  Her smooth round breast;
So he who has sorrow
  Shall have rest.
'XVIII', from *Chamber Music*

ΔOΞA EN YΨIΣTOIΣ ΘE

religion and *sin*

It is a curious thing, do you know, Cranly said
dispassionately, how your mind is supersaturated with the
religion in which you say you disbelieve.

A Portrait of the Artist as a Young Man

He is cured by faith who is sick of fate.

Finnegans Wake

The snares of the world were its ways of sin. He would
fall. He had not yet fallen but he would fall silently, in an
instant. Not to fall was too hard, too hard; and he felt the
silent lapse of his soul, as it would be at some instant to
come, falling, falling, but not yet fallen, still unfallen, but
about to fall.

A Portrait of the Artist as a Young Man

—This fire before us, said the dean, will be pleasing to the
eye. Will it therefore be beautiful?
—In so far as it is apprehended by the sight ... it will be
beautiful. ... In so far as it satisfies the animal craving for
warmth fire is a good. In hell, however, it is an evil.

A Portrait of the Artist as a Young Man

Phall if you but will, rise you must: and none so soon either shall the pharce for the nunce come to a setdown secular phoenish.

Finnegans Wake

Come on you winefizzling ginsizzling booseguzzling existences! Come on, you dog-gone, bullnecked,beetlebrowed, hogjowled, peanutbrained, weaseleyed fourflushers, false alarms and excess baggage! Come on, you triple extract of infamy! … The Deity aint no nickel dime bumshow. I put it to you that He's on the square and a corking fine business proposition. He's the grandest thing yet and don't you forget it. Shout salvation in King Jesus. You'll need to rise precious early, you sinner there, if you want to diddle the Almighty God.

Ulysses

If a man had stolen a pound in his youth and had used that pound to amass a huge fortune how much was he obliged to give back, the pound he had stolen only or the pound together with the compound interest accruing upon it or all his huge fortune? If a layman in giving baptism pour the water before saying the words is the child baptized? Is baptism with a mineral water valid? How comes it that while the first beatitude promises the kingdom of heaven

to the poor of heart the second beatitude promises also
to the meek that they shall possess the land? Why was
the sacrament of the eucharist instituted under the two
species of bread and wine if Jesus Christ be present body
and blood, soul and divinity, in the bread alone and in
the wine alone? Does a tiny particle of the consecrated
bread contain all the body and blood of Jesus Christ or a
part only of the body and blood? If the wine change into
vinegar and the host crumble into corruption after they
have been consecrated, is Jesus Christ still present under
their species as God and as man?

A Portrait of the Artist as a Young Man

In the name of Annah the Allmaziful, the Everliving, the
Bringer of Plurabilities, haloed be her eve, her singtime
sung, her rill be run, unhemmed as it is uneven!

Finnegans Wake

The preacher's knife had probed deeply into his disclosed
conscience and he felt now that his soul was festering in
sin. Yes, the preacher was right. God's turn had come.
Like a beast in its lair his soul had lain down in its own
filth but the blasts of the angel's trumpet had driven
him forth from the darkness of sin into the light. The
words of doom cried by the angel shattered in an instant

his presumptuous peace. The wind of the last day blew
through his mind, his sins, the jewel-eyed harlots of his
imagination, fled before the hurricane, squeaking like
mice in their terror and huddled under a mane of hair.

A Portrait of the Artist as a Young Man

The causes of his embitterment were many, remote and
near. He was angry with himself for being young and the prey
of restless foolish impulses, angry also with the change of
fortune which was reshaping the world about him into a vision
of squalor and insincerity. Yet his anger lent nothing to the
vision. He chronicled with patience what he saw, detaching
himself from it and tasting its mortifying flavour in secret.

A Portrait of the Artist as a Young Man

They used to go upstairs together on tiptoe, each with a
candle, and on the third landing exchange reluctant good-
nights. They used to kiss. He remembered well her eyes,
the touch of her hand and his delirium...

But delirium passes. He echoed her phrase, applying it
to himself: "*What am I to do?*" The instinct of the celibate
warned him to hold back. But the sin was there; even his
sense of honour told him that reparation must be made
for such a sin.

'The Boarding House', *Dubliners*

—Do you believe in the eucharist? Cranly asked.

—I do not, Stephen said.

—Do you disbelieve then?

—I neither believe in it nor disbelieve in it, Stephen answered.

—Many persons have doubts, even religious persons, yet they overcome them or put them aside, Cranly said. Are your doubts on that point too strong?

—I do not wish to overcome them, Stephen answered.

A Portrait of the Artist as a Young Man

Jesus Christ was not a hard taskmaster. He understood our little failings, understood the weakness of our poor fallen nature, understood the temptations of this life. We might have had, we all had from time to time, our temptations: we might have, we all had, our failings. But one thing only, he said, he would ask of his hearers. And that was: to be straight and manly with God. If their accounts tallied in every point to say:

"Well, I have verified my accounts. I find all well."

But if, as might happen, there were some discrepancies, to admit the truth, to be frank and say like a man:

"Well, I have looked into my accounts. I find this wrong and this wrong. But, with God's grace, I will rectify this and this. I will set right my accounts."

'Grace', *Dubliners*

Time was to sin and to enjoy, time was to scoff at God and at the warnings of His holy church, time was to defy His majesty, to disobey His commands, to hoodwink one's fellow men, to commit sin after sin and to hide one's corruption from the sight of men.

A Portrait of the Artist as a Young Man

He turned to appease the fierce longings of his heart before which everything else was idle and alien. He cared little that he was in mortal sin, that his life had grown to be a tissue of subterfuge and falsehood. Beside the savage desire within him to realize the enormities which he brooded on nothing was sacred. He bore cynically with the shameful details of his secret riots in which he exulted to defile with patience whatever image had attracted his eyes. By day and by night he moved among distorted images of the outer world. A figure that had seemed to him by day demure and innocent came towards him by night through the winding darkness of sleep, her face transfigured by a lecherous cunning, her eyes bright with brutish joy. Only the morning pained him with its dim memory of dark orgiastic riot, its keen and humiliating sense of transgression.

A Portrait of the Artist as a Young Man

Some people, says Bloom, can see the mote in others' eyes but they can't see the beam in their own.

Ulysses

Jesus Christ, with His divine understanding of every cranny of our human nature, understood that all men were not called to the religious life, that by far the vast majority were forced to live in the world, and, to a certain extent, for the world …

'Grace', *Dubliners*

His brain was simmering and bubbling within the cracking tenement of the skull. Flames burst forth from his skull like a corolla, shrieking like voices:

—Hell! Hell! Hell! Hell! Hell!

A Portrait of the Artist as a Young Man

His eyes were dimmed with tears and, looking humbly up to heaven, he wept for the innocence he had lost.

A Portrait of the Artist as a Young Man

"But though there were different names for God in all the different languages in the world and God understood what all the people who prayed said in their different languages, still God remained always the same God and

God's real name was God.

A Portrait of the Artist as a Young Man

… a darkness shining in brightness which brightness could not comprehend.

Ulysses

In the name of the former and of the latter and of their holo-caust.

Allmen.

Finnegans Wake

—We go to the house of God, Mr Casey said, in all humility to pray to our Maker and not to hear election addresses.

—It is religion, Dante said again. They are right. They must direct their flocks.

—And preach politics from the altar, is it? asked Mr Dedalus.

—Certainly, said Dante. It is a question of public morality. A priest would not be a priest if he did not tell his flock what is right and what is wrong.

A Portrait of the Artist as a Young Man

The fall (bababadalgharaghtakamminarronnkonnbronnto nner-ronntuonnthunntrovarrhounawnskawntoohoohoo

rdenenthur — nuk!) of a once wallstrait oldparr is retaled
early in bed and later on life down through all christian
minstrelsy.

Finnegans Wake

His blood was in revolt. He wandered up and down the
dark slimy streets peering into the gloom of lanes and
doorways, listening eagerly for any sound. He moaned to
himself like some baffled prowling beast. He wanted to sin
with another of his kind, to force another being to sin with
him and to exult with her in sin.

A Portrait of the Artist as a Young Man

A certain pride, a certain awe, withheld him from offering
to God even one prayer at night, though he knew it was in
God's power to take away his life while he slept and hurl his
soul hellward ere he could beg for mercy. His pride in his
own sin, his loveless awe of God, told him that his offence
was too grievous to be atoned for in whole or in part by a
false homage to the All-seeing and All-knowing.

A Portrait of the Artist as a Young Man

Till tree from tree, tree among trees tree over tree become
stone to stone, stone between stones, stone under stone
for ever.

O Loud, hear the wee beseech of thees of each of these thy
unlitten ones! Grant sleep in hour's time, O Loud!
That they take no chill. That they do ming no merder.
That they shall not gomeet madhowiatrees.
Loud, heap miseries upon us yet entwine our arts with
laugh-ters low!

Finnegans Wake

He had to undress and then kneel and say his own prayers
and be in bed before the gas was lowered so that he might
not go to hell when he died.

A Portrait of the Artist as a Young Man

Consider then what must be the foulness of the air of hell.
Imagine some foul and putrid corpse that has lain rotting
and decomposing in the grave, a jelly-like mass of liquid
corruption. Imagine such a corpse a prey to flames, devoured
by the fire of burning brimstone and giving off dense choking
fumes of nauseous loathsome decomposition. And then
imagine this sickening stench, multiplied a millionfold and
a millionfold again from the millions upon millions of fetid
carcasses massed together in the reeking darkness, a huge and
rotting human fungus. Imagine all this, and you will have
some idea of the horror of the stench of hell.

A Portrait of the Artist as a Young Man

Could it be that he, Stephen Dedalus, had done those things? His conscience sighed in answer. Yes, he had done them, secretly, filthily, time after time, and, hardened in sinful impenitence, he had dared to wear the mask of holiness before the tabernacle itself while his soul within was a living mass of corruption. How came it that God had not struck him dead?

A Portrait of the Artist as a Young Man

You find my words dark. Darkness is in our souls do you not think? ... Our souls, shamewounded by our sins, cling to us yet more, a woman to her lover clinging, the more the more.

Ulysses

generation is growing up in our midst, a generation actuated by new ideas and new principles...

it is also ... stood on the ...

ation ...

of the ...

Kind ... Stephen ... Stephen sa ...

the squea ...

Ulysses ... guarding as ever the waters of

there streamed forth at times upon the stillness the voice of prayer to her w...

es

history, politics and ireland

ciples. It is serious and enthusiastic for these new ideas and its enthusiasm, ev

for ireland!
a painted bridge
star

too fleeting day lingered lovingly

shore and, last but not least, on the c

radiance ... ossed heart of man, Mary, star of the

I'm deuced glad, I can tell you, to get back to the old
country. Does a fellow good, a bit of a holiday. I feel a ton
better since I landed again in dear dirty Dublin....

'A Little Cloud', *Dubliners*

"A new generation is growing up in our midst, a
generation actuated by new ideas and new principles.
It is serious and enthusiastic for these new ideas and its
enthusiasm, even when it is misdirected, is, I believe,
in the main sincere. But we are living in a sceptical and,
if I may use the phrase, a thought-tormented age: and
sometimes I fear that this new generation, educated or
hypereducated as it is, will lack those qualities of humanity,
of hospitality, of kindly humour which belonged to an
older day."

'The Dead', *Dubliners*

—If we could only live on good food like that, he said to
her somewhat loudly, we wouldn't have the country full of
rotten teeth and rotten guts. Living in a bogswamp, eating
cheap food and the streets paved with dust, horsedung and
consumptives' spits.

Ulysses

It was his habit to walk swiftly in the street even by day and whenever he found himself in the city late at night he hurried on his way apprehensively and excitedly. Sometimes, however, he courted the causes of his fear. He chose the darkest and narrowest streets and, as he walked boldly forward, the silence that was spread about his footsteps troubled him, the wandering, silent figures troubled him; and at times a sound of low fugitive laughter made him tremble like a leaf.

'A Little Cloud', *Dubliners*

"And haven't you your own land to visit," continued Miss Ivors, "that you know nothing of, your own people, and your own country?"

"O, to tell you the truth," retorted Gabriel suddenly, "I'm sick of my own country, sick of it!"

"Why?" asked Miss Ivors.

Gabriel did not answer for his retort had heated him.

"Why?" repeated Miss Ivors.

They had to go visiting together and, as he had not answered her, Miss Ivors said warmly:

"Of course, you've no answer."

'The Dead', *Dubliners*

I'm, he resumed, with dramatic force, as good an Irishman as that rude person I told you about at the outset and I want to see everyone, concluded he, all creeds and classes *pro rata* having a comfortable tidysized income... I call that patriotism.

Ulysses

I feel more strongly with every recurring year that our country has no tradition which does it so much honour and which it should guard so jealously as that of its hospitality. It is a tradition that is unique as far as my experience goes (and I have visited not a few places abroad) among the modern nations. Some would say, perhaps, that with us it is rather a failing than anything to be boasted of. But granted even that, it is, to my mind, a princely failing, and one that I trust will long be cultivated among us. Of one thing, at least, I am sure. As long as this one roof shelters the good ladies aforesaid – and I wish from my heart it may do so for many and many a long year to come – the tradition of genuine warm-hearted courteous Irish hospitality, which our forefathers have handed down to us and which we in turn must hand down to our descendants, is still alive among us ..."

'The Dead', *Dubliners*

We are an unfortunate priest-ridden race and always were and always will be ...

A Portrait of the Artist as a Young Man

No God for Ireland! he cried. We have had too much God In Ireland. Away with God!

A Portrait of the Artist as a Young Man

What birds were they? He stood on the steps of the library to look at them, leaning wearily on his ashplant. They flew round and round the jutting shoulder of a house in Molesworth Street. The air of the late March evening made clear their flight, their dark quivering bodies flying clearly against the sky as against a limp-hung cloth of smoky tenuous blue.

He watched their flight; bird after bird: a dark flash, a swerve, a flutter of wings. He tried to count them before all their darting quivering bodies passed: six, ten, eleven: and wondered were they odd or even in number. Twelve, thirteen: for two came wheeling down from the upper sky. They were flying high and low but ever round and round in straight and curving lines and ever flying from left to right, circling about a temple of air.

He listened to the cries: like the squeak of mice behind the wainscot: a shrill twofold note. But the notes were long and shrill and whirring, unlike the cry of vermin, falling a third or a fourth and trilled as the flying beaks clove the air. Their cry was shrill and clear and fine and falling like threads of silken light unwound from whirring spools.

A Portrait of the Artist as a Young Man

—Liquids I can eat, Stephen said. But O, oblige me by taking away that knife. I can't look at the point of it. It reminds me of Roman history.

Ulysses

The movements which work revolutions in the world are born out of the dreams and visions in a peasant's heart on the hillside. For them the earth is not an exploitable ground but the living mother.

Ulysses

—History, Stephen said, is a nightmare from which I am trying to awake.

Ulysses

There was no doubt about it: if you wanted to succeed you had to go away. You could do nothing in Dublin.

'A Little Cloud', *Dubliners*

This race and this country and this life produced me, he said I shall express myself as I am.

A Portrait of the Artist as a Young Man

—Kingstown pier, Stephen said. Yes, a disappointed bridge.

Ulysses

Good puzzle would be cross Dublin without passing a pub.

Ulysses

The summer evening had begun to fold the world in its mysterious embrace. Far away in the west the sun was setting and the last glow of all too fleeting day lingered lovingly on sea and strand, on the proud promontory of dear old Howth guarding as ever the waters of the bay, on the weedgrown rocks along Sandymount shore and, last but not least, on the quiet church whence there streamed forth at times upon the stillness the voice of prayer to her who is in her pure radiance a beacon ever to the stormtossed heart of man, Mary, star of the sea.

Ulysses

The snotgreen sea. The scrotumtightening sea.

Ulysses

I hear an army charging upon the land,
    And the thunder of horses plunging, foam about their knees:
Arrogant, in black armour, behind them stand,
    Disdaining the reins, with fluttering whips, the charioteers.

They cry unto the night their battle-name:
    I moan in sleep when I hear afar their whirling laughter.
They cleave the gloom of dreams, a blinding flame,
    Clanging, clanging upon the heart as upon an anvil.

They come shaking in triumph their long, green hair:
    They come out of the sea and run shouting by the shore.
My heart, have you no wisdom thus to despair?
    My love, my love, my love, why have you left me alone?

'XXXVI' from *Chamber Music*

mortality and time

are always in ... gatherings such as this ... der thou ...

... are always in gatherings such as this ... der thou ...

Ulysses

'The Dead' Dubliners

His soul swooned slowly as he heard the snow
falling faintly through the universe and faintly falling, like the
descent of their last end, upon all the living and the dead.

'The Dead' Dubliners

descent of their last end, upon all the living and the dead.

I was happier then. Or was that I? Or am I now I? … Can't
bring back time. Like holding water in your hand. Would
you go back to then? Just beginning then. Would you?

Ulysses

Know all men, he said, time's ruins build eternity's
mansions. What means this?

Ulysses

… there is a future in every past that is present

Finnegans Wake

He had not died but he had faded out like a film in the
sun. He had been lost or had wandered out of existence for
he no longer existed. How strange to think of him passing
out of existence in such a way, not by death but by fading
out in the sun or by being lost and forgotten somewhere in
the universe!

A Portrait of the Artist as a Young Man

"… there are always in gatherings such as this sadder
thoughts that will recur to our minds: thoughts of the past,
of youth, of changes, of absent faces that we miss here
tonight. Our path through life is strewn with many such
sad memories: and were we to brood upon them always we

could not find the heart to go on bravely with our work among the living. We have all of us living duties and living affections which claim, and rightly claim, our strenuous endeavours.

"Therefore, I will not linger on the past. I will not let any gloomy moralising intrude upon us here tonight. Here we are gathered together for a brief moment from the bustle and rush of our everyday routine. We are met here as friends, in the spirit of good-fellowship, as colleagues, also to a certain extent, in the true spirit of camaraderie ..."
'The Dead', *Dubliners*

Eternity! O, dread and dire word. Eternity! What mind of man can understand it?
A Portrait of the Artist as a Young Man

Therefore, everyman, look to that last end that is thy death and the dust that gripeth on every man that is born of woman for as he came naked forth from his mother's womb so naked shall he wend him at the last for to go as he came.
Ulysses

It is as painful perhaps to be awakened from a vision as to be born.
Ulysses

The oaks of ald now they lie in peat yet elms leap where askes lay.

Finnegans Wake

If he had smiled why would he have smiled?

To reflect that each one who enters imagines himself to be the first to enter whereas he is always the last term of a preceding series even if the first term of a succeeding one, each imagining himself to be first, last, only and alone whereas, he is neither first nor last nor only nor alone in a series originating in and repeated to infinity.

Ulysses

Though Wonderlawn's lost us for ever. Alis, alas, she broke the glass! Liddell lokker through the leafery, ours is mistery of pain.

Finnegans Wake

One by one they were all becoming shades. Better pass boldly into that other world, in the full glory of some passion, than fade and wither dismally with age. He thought of how she who lay beside him had locked in her heart for so many years that image of her lover's eyes when he had told her that he did not wish to live.

Generous tears filled Gabriel's eyes. He had never felt

like that himself towards any woman but he knew that such a feeling must be love. The tears gathered more thickly in his eyes and in the partial darkness he imagined he saw a form of a young man standing under a dripping tree. Other forms were near. His soul had approached that region where dwell the vast hosts of the dead. He was conscious of, but could not apprehend, their wayward and flickering existence. His own identity was fading out into a grey impalpable world: the solid world itself which these dead had one time reared and lived in was dissolving and dwindling.

A few light taps upon the pane made him turn to the window. It had begun to snow again. He watched sleepily the flakes, silver and dark, falling obliquely against the lamplight. The time had come for him to set out on his journey westward. Yes, the newspapers were right: snow was general all over Ireland. It was falling on every part of the dark central plain, on the treeless hills, falling softly on the Bog of Allen and, further westward, softly falling into the dark mutinous Shannon waves. It was falling, too, upon every part of the lonely churchyard on the hill where Michael Furey lay buried. It lay thickly drifted on the crooked crosses and headstones, on the spears of the little gate, on the barren thorns. His soul swooned slowly as he heard the snow falling faintly through the universe and faintly falling, like the descent of their last end, upon all the living and the dead.

'The Dead', *Dubliners*

They lived und laughed ant loved end left.

Finnegans Wake

"Did he … peacefully?" she asked.

"Oh, quite peacefully, ma'am," said Eliza. "You couldn't tell when the breath went out of him. He had a beautiful death, God be praised."

"And everything…?"

"Father O'Rourke was in with him a Tuesday and anointed him and prepared him and all.

"He knew then?"

"He was quite resigned."

"He looks quite resigned," said my aunt.

"That's what the woman we had in to wash him said. She said he just looked as if he was asleep, he looked that peaceful and resigned. No one would think he'd make such a beautiful corpse."

'The Sisters', *Dubliners*

—The most profound sentence ever written, Temple said
with enthusiasm, is the sentence at the end of the zoology.
Reproduction is the beginning of death.

A Portrait of the Artist as a Young Man

And when all was said and done, the lies a fellow told about
himself couldn't probably hold a proverbial candle to the
wholesale whoppers other fellows coined about him.

Ulysses

—Full many a flower is born to blush unseen.

Ulysses

He watched the scene and thought of life; and (as always
happened when he thought of life) he became sad. A gentle
melancholy took possession of him. He felt how useless it
was to struggle against fortune, this being the burden of
wisdom which the ages had bequeathed to him.

'A Little Cloud' *Dubliners*

I am, a stride at a time. A very short space of time through
very short times of space.

Ulysses

Bury the dead. Say Robinson Crusoe was true to life. Well then Friday buried him. Every Friday buries a Thursday if you come to look at it.

Ulysses

Read your own obituary notice they say you live longer. Gives you second wind. New lease of life.

Ulysses

When one reads these strange pages of one long gone one feels that one is at one with one who once ...

Ulysses

There was cold sunlight outside the window. He wondered if he would die. You could die just the same on a sunny day.

A Portrait of the Artist as a Young Man

How many! All these here once walked round Dublin. Faithful departed. As you are now so once were we.

Ulysses

With what meditations did Bloom accompany his demonstration to his companion of various constellations?

Meditations of evolution increasingly vaster: of the

moon invisible in incipient lunation, approaching perigee: of the infinite lattiginous scintillating uncondensed milky way, discernible by daylight by an observer placed at the lower end of a cylindrical vertical shaft 5000 ft deep sunk from the surface towards the centre of the earth: of Sirius (alpha in Canis Maior) 10 lightyears (57,000,000,000,000 miles) distant and in volume 900 times the dimension of our planet: of Arcturus: of the precession of equinoxes: of Orion with belt and sextuple sun theta and nebula in which 100 of our solar systems could be contained: of moribund and of nascent new stars such as Nova in 1901: of our system plunging towards the constellation of Hercules: of the parallax or parallactic drift of socalled fixed stars, in reality evermoving wanderers from immeasurably remote eons to infinitely remote futures in comparison with which the years, threscore and ten, of allotted human life formed a parenthesis of infinitesimal brevity.

Ulysses

The past is consumed in the present and the present is living only because it brings forth the future.

A Portrait of the Artist as a Young Man

Poor Aunt Julia! She, too, would soon be a shade with the shade of Patrick Morkan and his horse. He had caught that haggard look upon her face for a moment when she was singing *Arrayed for the Bridal*. Soon, perhaps, he would be sitting in that same drawing-room, dressed in black, his silk hat on his knees. The blinds would be drawn down and Aunt Kate would be sitting beside him, crying and blowing her nose and telling him how Julia had died. He would cast about in his mind for some words that might console her, and would find only lame and useless ones ...

'The Dead', *Dubliners*

He was alone. He was unheeded, happy and near to the wild heart of life. He was alone and young and wilful and wildhearted, alone amid a waste of wild air and brackish waters and the sea-harvest of shells and tangle and veiled grey sunlight and gayclad lightclad figures of children and girls and voices childish and girlish in the air.

A Portrait of the Artist as a Young Man

Hold to the now, the here, through which all future plunges to the past.

Ulysses

Gentle lady, do not sing
  Sad songs about the end of love;
Lay aside sadness and sing
  How love that passes is enough.

Sing about the long deep sleep
  Of lovers that are dead, and how
In the grave all love shall sleep:
  Love is aweary now.

'XXVIII', from *Chamber Music*

DESIGNER'S NOTE

Best-Loved Joyce is an exploration of the work of a writer of enormous empathy and compassion who celebrated all things human.

With Joyce it is challenging to create illustrative material because the work encompasses so much. I worked with the idea of reducing all to an incessant 'layering of meaning' – and emphasising the sense of place. Dublin is reflected again and again in his work. By combining the text of each section with a relevant image of Dublin, I created 'landscape typographic paintings'. The words in their abstraction become part of the landscape, maybe the sea, or the sky or part of the road.

The first edition of 1,000 copies of *Ulysses* appeared in blue wrappers. The shade of blue is often described as Aegean Sea, Greek flag blue, in keeping with Homer's *Odyssey*. The shade is mirrored here in this volume of quotations.

The typographic paintings are largely constructed with Helvetica, the ultimate modernist font, resonating with Joyce as the great modernist, but I also use a classic serif, Mrs Eaves, to link a more romantic idea of landscape, also a nod towards the duality of people and place. The drawings within these landscapes are very loose, sketchy and almost 'dirty', to give an impressionistic look to the work. I think this creates atmosphere, and draws you into the words. They are based on photographs and prints that were contemporary in Joyce's time. *Truth* incorporates a drawing of Grattan's Parliament, *Love and Romance* is an image of The Bailey Lighthouse at Howth; *Family and Domestic Life* shows O'Connell Street; *Art Literature and Music* is Kingstown (Dun Laoghaire) Pier; *Living* is a drawing based on a print of the Phoenix Park; *Desire and Sex* show Mount Jerome cemetery; *Religion and Sin* depicts St George's Church at Hardwicke Place; *History Politics and Ireland* is based on a photograph of George V's visit to Kingstown; and finally the famous Ballast Office clock forms the basis of *Mortality and Time*.

Emma Byrne